A LOOK AT LEWES

THE HIGH STREET OF LEWES

From St. Anne's Church to Lewes Bridge

FROM ORIGINAL DRAWINGS
BY JOHN HOUGHTON

Tartarus Press, 1998

A Look at Lewes
by John Houghton
© John Houghton, 1998

First published by
Tartarus Press, 1998
at 5 Birch Terrace, Hangingbirch Lane
Horam, East Sussex, TN21 OPA.

Printed by Print Matters, Hailsham, Sussex.

ISBN 1872621 39 2

Introduction

Eighteen years ago I started drawing the buildings of Lewes High Street between Westgate Street and Eastgate Street, based on my own research and observation. This work originated from my study of the illustrations in Walter Godfrey's book *Our Building Inheritance* (Readers Union and Faber and Faber, 1946). Many of the buildings have remained unchanged since his time, so there will be a similarity between his and my work, but there have been some alterations. During the last two years I have added the areas from Westgate Street to St Anne's church, and from Eastgate Street to the Bridge. In a few cases I have inset details from Godfrey's drawings for buildings that have disappeared, but these have been acknowledged as his work.

Mine are architectural drawings, rather than architects' drawings. They are at a consistent horizontal scale, but there may be some small inconsistencies in the vertical scale.

In the main, Lewes High Street comprises houses with Georgian fronts, but these often disguise Tudor structures which may stand on medieval undercrofts. The drawings show the appearance of buildings up to the end of the nineteenth century, with only a few of the twentieth century.

The information in the text, based on my own research, may well conflict with the work of others. Copies of all my underlying research into property ownership are deposited in the East Sussex County Record Office and in the Library at Barbican House.

Readers who wish to know about the more recent occupancy of any building are recommended to use the various street directories (e.g. *Kelly's Directory*) available in the County Library. There are many other sources of information. I commend to your attention particularly the various works of Walter Godfrey, Les Davey and Colin Brent, who have covered all or parts of the same subject.

John Houghton, 1998

Conventions.

Doors in most cases are shown as empty spaces without detail. The scale is too small to do justice to the many fine doorcases.

Shop windows may be shown blank where there is no record of the past appearance.

Chimney Stacks are not always shown, and where they are, have been simplified.

SHEET ONE
Lewes High Street, from Lewes Bridge to Friars Walk.

This area has suffered much demolition and re-building so the treatment here is different from the rest. The illustrations show buildings in a variety of conditions. Outline drawings show the position and bulk of the present buildings. The extent to which the buildings draw their architectural derivation from the style of No. 223 opposite (see sheet two), or The Tabernacle, can be seen.

<u>TOP LINE . South side. left to right (Bridge to Friars Walk)</u>
The whole frontage was held of the Crown by the Convent of Grey Friars until the dissolution.
Riverside is a warehouse dating to the late eighteenth/early nineteenth centuries, rented from the owners of the Friars by a number of tenants, and was the site of the Town Wharf in 1675. Behind here c.1855-92 was the Etna ironworks of C.A. Wells.
<u>Railway Lane</u> is followed by
No. 1. The first house in Lewes High Street. Sir Henry Blackman, the importing wine merchant, occupied the house and the Town wharf c.1790-1812.
Nos. 2-4. Site of The Tabernacle, (Congregational chapel) erected 1816, enlarged 1832 (as shown here). It was demolished in 1954, when the congregation moved to Prince Edward's Road.
Nos. 5-7. Late Georgian houses (not shown), built c.1812, demolished in 1868 to make way for the Lewes-Uckfield branch line railway.
Nos. 8-9. (Now not numbered as such). Greyfriars, a building of around 1673, of which Riverside may be a conscious copy. The estate was progressively broken up for development after 1803. Greyfriars was the place where King William IV and Queen Adelaide were entertained in 1830 by Nehemiah Wimble, the then owner. It was demolished before the construction of the first Railway Station in 1846.
Nos. 9-10 (now 10 only). Fitzroy House. Built 1862 to a design by Sir Gilbert Scott as a memorial library to Hon. Henry Fitzroy, MP for Lewes. It became a financial liability for his widow and was taken over by the Borough Council in 1872. The local authority had agreed to demolish the whole structure, but it was rescued for the town by the present occupier.

<u>Inset</u>
The first Lewes Railway Station, in Friars Walk behind Fitzroy House. Regarded as almost useless from the time it was built in 1846, it was used as a goods depot. It is a shame that we have now lost this building which was demolished in the 1960s.

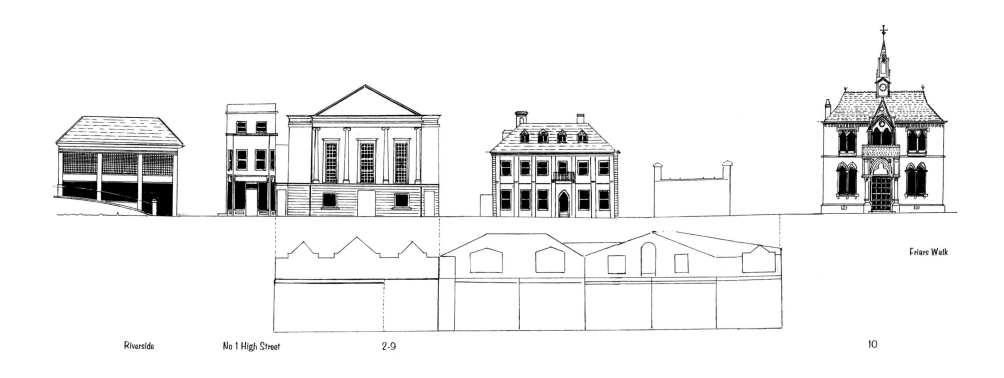

Riverside   No 1 High Street   2-9   10

Friars Walk

Old Railway Station
(In Friars Walk)

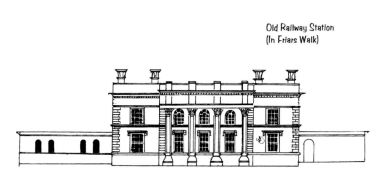

3

SHEET TWO. TOP LINE

High Street (School Hill) from No 211 to Lewes Bridge

Nos. 211. Built before 1790. The beautiful brickwork is probably due to the use of brick 'slips'.

Nos. 212. Built before 1790, perhaps as early as 1720.

Nos. 213. Dates to 1607/8. The facade covers a gabled, timber-framed building, in the ownership of the Trayton family from c.1570 to 1770. This was the Town armoury, and home of the town's local commander during the Civil War. The front is clad with mathematical tiles.

Nos. 214. Site sold after 1790 and this building is mid eighteenth century. Said to be the site of Holy Trinity Church, but if this is here it is beneath the stone/brick/flint wall on the west side, which includes Caen stone at the lowest level.

BOTTOM LINE.

Nos. 215. This plot originated in a grant of copyhold from the waste of Lewes Manor around 1683. In about 1938 the buildings were demolished and Seveirg Buildings was erected in their place, subsequently to be demolished to make way for the present shopping precinct (shown in outline).

Nos. 216-9. Demolished in 1868 for the railway (the position of the bridge is shown). A replacement No. 219 (also shown) was subsequently constructed.

No. 216. Drops out of the historical record by 1874.

Nos. 220-1. Two houses in 1683, with a substantial land-holding broken up by 1825 for street nos. 216-219. The front (c.1740) is of Caen stone, and may have been obtained from the Friary 'wall' opposite and in Friars Walk. The house may have been modified by George Rickman, Quaker industrialist, in around 1807. The solicitors now in occupation originated here in 1871.

Nos. 223-4. Originally one house, of which no. 224 is a remnant. Most of the contents of nos. 223, including a fine stair, were removed and sold to the USA, and the house demolished c.1909, to allow for the present no. 223. The records for this plot go back to 1506-7.

4

211   212   213   214   Eastgate Street

215-8   Modern Eastgate Shopping Development   219   220/1   223   224

School Hill (High Street) from Friars Walk to Broomans Lane.

No. 11. A barn before 1756, converted subsequently to commercial and residential uses. It was bounded to the east by Church Lane, next to the Friary, and to the south by Puddle Wharf. Rebuilt in 1853 as Lewes Dispensary, forerunner of Lewes Victoria Hospital, and converted in 1925 for Lewes Building Society.

No. 13. (Has now subsumed no. 12). This has a Georgian brick front, and is said to have Elizabethan panelling inside.

No. 14. Later facade seems to contain an earlier building. Occupied 1776-1869 by Attwood & Wimble, ironfounders and engineers, who employed 35 men and 11 boys in 1871. Successors to the Attwood family of watchmakers.

No. 15. Re-built after a fire in 1958.

Nos. 16-16a. Richard Broughton (a successful cooper) lived here until c.1820 and gave it the name of Broughton House. The name was later used for a Ladies school. The present appearance presumably reflects ownership by the Prudential Assurance Co after 1920.

No. 17. The present building may be the Lewes Savings Bank of 1871.

Nos. 18, 18a, 19. First historical reference is 1683, but separate buildings by c.1777. The covered passage leads to further buildings and land behind.

Nos. 20/21. Was occupied from 1828 to 1882 by Thomas Hill, then by Misses Selina and Delia Hill, all bakers and pastrycooks. Re-built in 1892 by Caleb Mitchell, draper and undertaker.

BOTTOM LINE

Nos. 22-4. This was one property when first identified in 1504, currently of eighteenth century appearance. No. 22 was occupied from 1728 to 1933 by the Turner family, apothecaries, then general practitioners, finally as Turner, Crosskey and Dow (surgeons). Re-fronted 1938 by Lewes and District Electricity Supply Co. The gabled and tiled rear elevation betrays an earlier building. No. 23 is a re-building and probably dates from the time of Charles Gilbert (attorney) before 1790. John Farnes, a miller, lived here at no. 24. Richard Lambe (auctioneer) was the occupier 1812, having married Farnes' daughter.

Nos. 25-6. A post World War II replacement on part of an earlier, larger plot which was divided up in 1669. In 1680 this was the house where arms and munitions left over from the Civil War, were returned. It was the Unicorn Inn in c.1680, and Miss Lund had a ladies school here, which had moved from St Peter's church, Westout.

Nos. 27-9. The George & Dragon Coffee House occupies no. 29 in 1874, becoming a Temperance Hotel by 1881. Now a Victorian Gothic revival. Nos. 28 and 29 were built on land once occupied by All Saints' Almshouses (see nos. 30/31 below).

Nos. 30/1. Probably built after 1790 on the site of the Almshouses (see nos. 25/6 above). Occupied by chemists (Joseph Breeds and Charles Pitts, then Parkinson & Winton, then John Head) throughout the nineteenth century. Occupied by Chailey Rural District Council from the mid 1930s until post-war local government re-organisation.

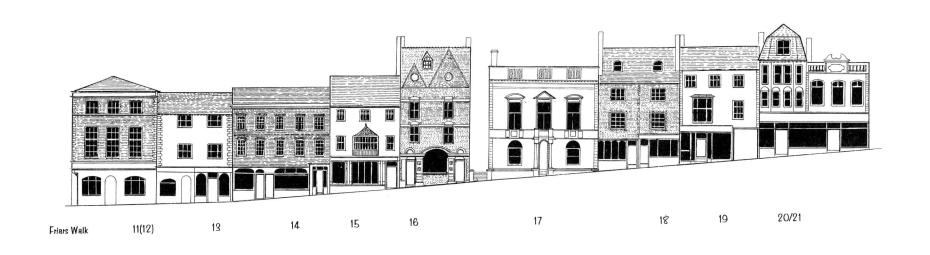

Friars Walk   11(12)   13   14   15   16   17   18   19   20/21

22   23   24   25/6   27   28   29   30/31

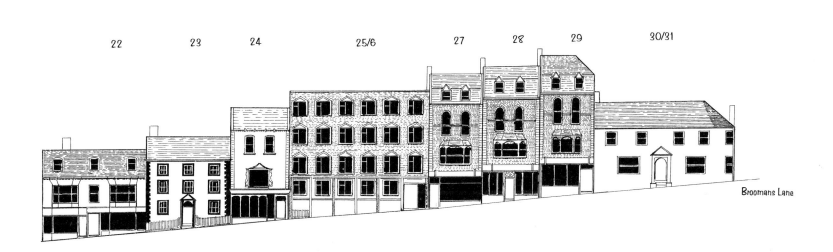

Broomans Lane

7

School Hill from Aylards Corner (Market Street) to no. 210 High Street.

Nos. 192-3. On the site of property held in 1513 by John Aylard, the origin of the name Aylard's Corner. Re-developed about 1822, and then again in 1891 to acheive its present appearance.

Nos. 194-200. Until 1789 this was one large property with substantial lands to the north. The present buildings date from that time.

Nos. 201-4. All of these properties were copyhold, and possibly represent the site of the earliest town walls, granted out in around 1580.

Nos. 201-2. These may have been divided in 1604, but their present appearance dates from after 1702. They are clad in mathematical tiles.

No. 203. Rebuilt in 1735. A fine property. No. 203 became freehold about 1607.

BOTTOM LINE

No. 204. The name School Hill Creamery records its occupation from 1922 by Albert John Reed, dairyman. Clad in slate tiles.

Nos. 205-6. An early post-medieval building of about 1540.

No. 207. Fake timber framing of concrete.

Nos. 208/9. Built in 1826 as part of the re-development of site of the Turks Head Inn, in conjunction with Albion Street.

Albion Street. Created c.1826

Albion House. Post World War II. Built on land of the Turks Head Inn.

No. 210. All Saints House. Probably built in 1855 by George Rigden. The right side was originally part of no. 211 next door. The left side was first built in 1769 on open land of the Turk's Head Inn.

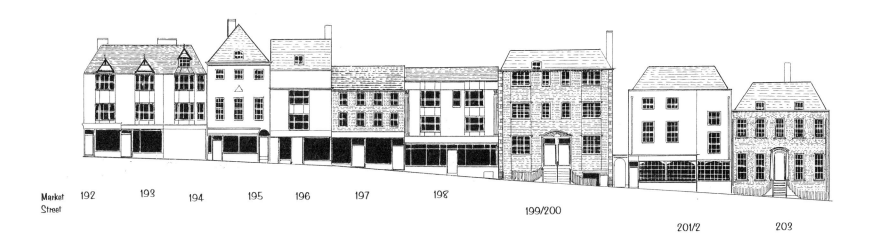

Market
Street
192
193
194
195
196
197
198
199/200
201/2
203

204
205/6
207
208
209
1 Albion Street
Albion Street
Albion House
210 (All Saints House)

9

SHEET FIVE. BOTTOM LINE
South side. from Broomans Lane to 53 High Street.

No. 32. Lewes House. A fine eighteenth century house, better appreciated from the rear. Nos. 32 and 33 can be traced back to 1609, but became divided in about 1704. The front was added after 1812. From 1890 to 1928 it was the home of American antiquarian and art buyer for American museums, E. Perry Warren, who commissioned a copy of Rodin's sculpture 'The Kiss', which scandalised the town.

No. 33. School Hill House. An important early eighteenth century building, built in 1715 by Dr Peter White after his purchase of an earlier house from William Thomas (d.1639), who had been Clerk of the Peace for Sussex. Later owned by John Fuller ('Honest John' or 'Mad Jack) 1753-1790.

No. 34. Once one property covering nos. 34-7, it was the White Lyon Inn by 1683. The timbered east wall of no. 34 may date from 1598 or before. Separated in 1808 by John Baxter, the stationer, tanner, and printer, founder of the Sussex Agricultural Express.

No. 35-7. John Baxter leased nos. 36 and 37 to John & Albion Russell (of Chiddingly & Lewes, bootmakers) who later became Russell & Bromley at no. 186 High Street.

Nos. 38-40. The two buildings brought together in 1938.

TOP LINE

No. 41. Its present appearance dates from the mid eighteenth century. The property was held in two major divisions, the southern part being held of the Manor of Southover.

St.Nicholas Lane

Nos. 42-4. Divided in three after 1624. Tudor work within, with some medieval details. Charles Pitt undertook the re-building of the chambers over the shop at the front in 1789/80, and the present upper front with a fine cast iron frieze dates from then. The date on the front may be the date of the seventeenth century division into three.

Nos. 45-7. These were re-built in 1800-2, and in 1812 were numbered 45/6, while street no. 47 was added to no. 48.

Nos. 47-8. Contained the Lewes Library Society up to 1818.

No. 49. Is a good timber-framed medieval building with a crown post roof.

Station Street

No. 50. Separated from no. 51 in about 1790, re-built around 1850.

Nos. 51/2. Records of this house go back to 1499. It was the Crown Inn between 1671-1680, then in 1683 the Pelicans, named after the Pelham family. John (1790), then Thomas Budgen (1812), cartographers, lived here, then Mark Anthony Lower (1828), who operated a circulating library and bookshop.

Nos. 53/4. One house, the last in St John sub Castro parish, a good sixteenth century timber building traceable to 1534. Behind is an even earlier one with a crown post roof, which originally over-looked the Market Place until no. 53 colonized forward. Bought by the Pelhams in 1577, it continued to be part of their extensive Lewes properties until 1840. The cartway to the White Hart yard was bridged over during the mid seventeenth century. The enlarged building then became the George Inn.

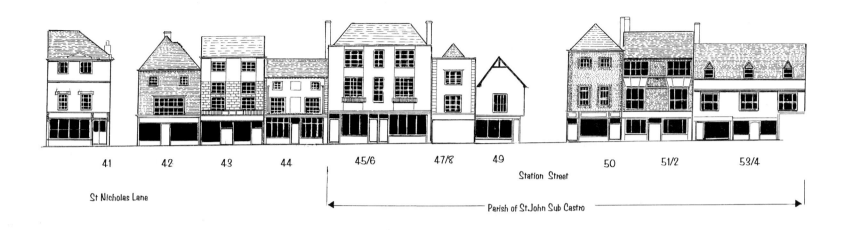

41   42   43   44   45/6   47/8   49   50   51/2   53/4

Station Street

St Nicholas Lane

Parish of St John Sub Castro

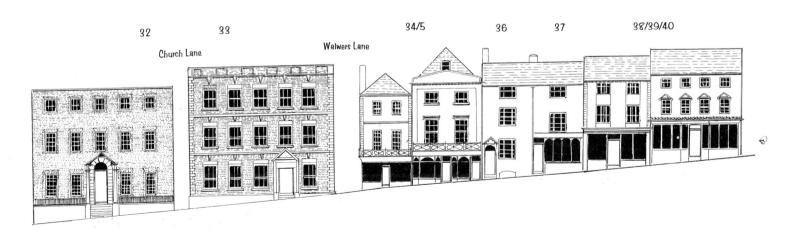

32   33   34/5   36   37   38/39/40

Church Lane   Walwers Lane

11

North side, from Pope's Entry to Market Street (Aylards Corner).

Pope's Entry was diverted onto this line after about 1736, up to which date it ran between nos. 179 and 180.

No. 179. Substantially re-built as the Rainbow Tavern c.1890

No. 180. Demolished by East Sussex County Council in 1929, to allow for the westwards extension of Newcastle House, then in use as the County Hall.

Nos. 181-2. Newcastle House. The pastiche of 1929 in Portland Stone replaced the building, shown in the drawing which was considered by some to have been the finest building in Lewes High Street. The drawing shows its appearance when built between 1679-1701 by William Pellatt. It was rented by Thomas Pelham-Holles, Duke of Newcastle, and used as a political coffee house around 1734.

(The modern boundary of the parishes of St Michaels and St John sub Castro now passes between Newcastle House and no. 183 (Once County Hall, now the Crown Courts). This change was made when the County Hall was built, in replacement of a number of small properties on the site.)

No. 183. County Hall, now the Crown Courts, built between 1808-1812 on a site held by the Pelham family. This replaced the older Town Hall and Sessions House, formerly situated in the middle of the High Street opposite.

Nos. 184-5. Held of the Manor of Ringmer, this property was the 'greater house' and wraps round into Fisher Street to include the 'lesser house'. It was the home and clock manufactory of William Attwood and his successors. Demolished in 1900 to make way for another extension to the County Hall.

No. 186. An enigmatic property, copyhold of the Manor of Lewes, a late grant reflecting the forward growth of buildings on the north side of the High Street, which left this at first as open space. Certainly built before c.1570, when it can first be identified in historical records. The front (at least) must have been re-built in the late eighteenth century.

BOTTOM LINE

No. 187/8. Another enigmatic copyhold. Traceable from 1570, it was the King's Arms before 1730, then the Star Coffee House until 1859, when it was sold to Albion Russell (later Russell & Bromley). The two numbers relate to the front and the back parts. Earlier illustrations show massive bow windows, traces of which remain in the basement.

No. 189. The Star Inn as rebuilt c.1739-44 by Thomas Sergison, and substantially altered in 1891-3 on conversion to Lewes Town Hall. Always held of the Manor of Southover, always a very prominent establishment in the history of the town.

Nos. 190-2. All held of Southover Manor,

No. 191. Keeling House (although it may have originally been 'Keating House'). Possibly re-built in 1839, and later occupied by Barclays Bank.

No. 192. The Black Lyon Inn in 1633-1745, then the Crown Inn in 1790. A possible re-building of 1811.

Market Tower. Built in 1791/2 (in part by Amon Wilds), but at that date free-standing.

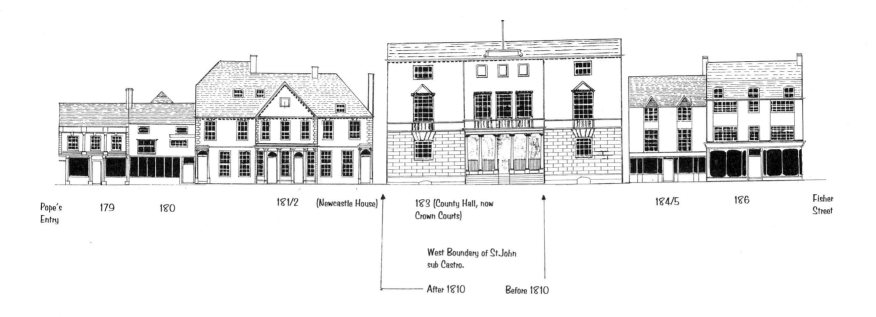

Pope's
Entry   179   180   181/2   (Newcastle House)   183 (County Hall, now   184/5   186   Fisher
                                                                Crown Courts)   Street

West Boundary of St.John
sub Castro.

After 1810   Before 1810

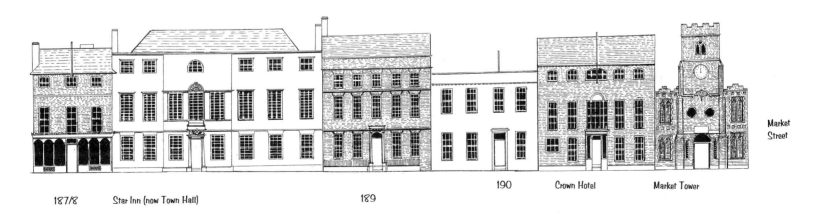

187/8   Star Inn (now Town Hall)   189   190   Crown Hotel   Market Tower   Market
                                                                                               Street

SHEET SEVEN. TOP LINE.

South side, from the White Hart to Stewards Inn.

No. 55. The White Hart. Can be dated back to 1525, but was bought by Thomas Pelham in 1568 as his town house. Richard Verrall lived here from 1727 as first master of the Inn.

Nos. 56-9. All these properties were part of the Pelham 'empire'. Nos. 56/7 Ccn be traced back to 1385. It became the Unicorn Inn , rebuilt between 1881-1905.

Nos. 58/9. The first reference dates to 1343, the earliest record found so far by the present writer. The Pelhams bought it in 1581. Dr James Moore lived here in 1803 before buying Castle Place. Nos. 57 and 8 were combined as a restaurant and had become Holloway's Restaurant by 1938.

St Andrews Lane.

No. 60. May have been held of the Manor of Southover. George Goring bought it in 1579 from a John Cottmott. This plot is blank on a map of 1775 which suggests that it was being re-built then.

Nos. 61 (a.b.&c). These were one property up to 1683 but can be traced back in part to c.1570, divided by 1787. The long frontage was then developed as one shop and warehouse. The fine shop front was removed in 1936 when Lowdell and Cooper went into liquidation, and later destroyed.

Nos. 62-3. Can be traced back to 1570-81. No. 63 was in the same ownership as nos. 62 and 64 in 1683. By 1874 it had become a land and estate agents and auctioneers (Chapman and Martin). It was rebuilt in its present form by London City and Midland Bank in 1936-8.

No. 64. The building is a replacement of 1842 after the destruction by fire of the premises of William Lee, bookseller, printer, publisher and editor of the Lewes Journal in 1753. Lee's business was continued by George Bacon (Sussex Advertiser) and the Southern Counties Press until about 1905 when it became the London & Provincial Bank, later Barclays. Land agent Martin moved here from no. 62 by 1938, and in partnership with Gorringe, formed Rowland Gorringe & Co, still here. The inset drawing (based on Walter Godfrey) shows how it used to look, with Watergate Lane wider than now.

BOTTOM LINE. Watergate Lane

Nos. 65/6. A pair, of which the eastern half was once a mirror image of the western half. No. 65 was a ladies boarding school from about 1855. By 1871 this had moved to the rear and had become a Quaker school. The Post Office began here in 1881 as A. Morris, Bookseller and Post Office.

No. 67. Rebuilt c.1909, seemingly as a pastiche claimed to date from the fourteenth century.

Nos. 68/9. Replaces an earlier building demolished c.1938

Nos. 70-73. The earliest record shows this as one building, later divided into four. No. 73 had a westward extension over St Martin's Lane, since removed.

St.Martin's Lane

Nos. 74-6. This was the Stewards Inn of the Barony of Lewes. No. 74-5 is certainly fourteenth century and probably the oldest surviving building in Lewes. George Randoll, a Lewes map maker in the early seventeenth century, lived here. No. 76 is part of it, but its frontage is eighteenth century.

Nos. 77. Probably the site of or access way for the stables of Steward's Inn. It may have been built in 1777. (There is a dated brick beside the staircase.)

55   56   57   58   59   St Andrew's 60   61 a   b   c   62   63   64
                                        Lane

Watergate
Lane

65   66   67   68 69   70   71   72   73   St.Martin's   74/5   76   77
                                              Lane

15

North side, from St Michael's church to Pope's Entry.

<u>St Michael's Church.</u> The drawing shows the church before the small chancel was added in 1878, and before the earlier clock house was demolished. Tom Paine was married here. The quality of the knapped flint work, of about 1748 is especially fine.

Nos. 159-60. Once copyhold, occupied by Thomas Reeves, photographer, probably the oldest established commercial photographer anywhere in the UK, from 1871. Refronted during the eighteenth century.

Nos. 161-2. The owners can be traced back to 1542. This was later another Pelham property, and Cater Rand, surveyor and schoolmaster, was at no. 162 from about 1781 until made bankrupt in 1808. No. 161 was the Lewes Constabulary Office from 1881.

Nos. 163-4. The central way (closed in the nineteenth century) was once a public highway, but the building dates from before 1542, when the western part was sold into separate ownership.

Nos. 165-7 From before 1600 this was the 'White Horse' Inn, which continued until c.1730 or later. It was pulled down and four houses erected in its place in 1812-15. Dr James Moore bought the central pair (hence the current three street numbers). Amon Wilds was commissioned to design the new buildings, and he re-designed the facade with his signature 'Ammonite' capitals on pilasters. Gideon Mantell, doctor and geologist) later became James Moore's partner.

No. 168. Was the home of the Jefferies family (there is a large memorial in Chiddingly Church) and then of Dodson, goldsmiths, from 1612 to 1674. By 1683 it adjoined the Market House. This is one of Lewes' many buildings clad in mathematical tiles, hung in about 1803 to dress up the earlier timber frame building.

<u>Castle Gate</u>

BOTTOM LINE

No. 169. Barbican House. Now the museum of the Sussex Archaeological Society, bought in 1908. A substantial timber-framed building dating to before 1525, encased in a later brickwork shell. The south-western angle has a 'dragon beam', similar to the north-eastern angle of no. 75 opposite.

No. 170. Destroyed by fire in 1907. Miss Louisa Lee (later the Misses Rudgwick) had a boys preparatory boarding school here c.1843-1881.

Nos. 171-2. Given to the Town by Thomas Blunt, barber-surgeon in 1611. Taken down and re-built in 1759.

Nos. 174-5. One building in single occupation up to c.1560, when Richard Ball sold it in two parts. A classic sixteenth century building. Thomas Dicker, one of the founders of Lewes (Old) Bank, lived in no. 175 in 1793.

Nos. 176/7. These were owned by the Matthews, (butchers and substantial property owners in Lewes) from 1602 to 1705. No. 176 sold to Charles Verrall in 1805, who re-developed it as separate properties, continuing to occupy no. 177 himself.

No. 178. With no. 179, this was originally one house, now much re-built. The division and re-building seems to have been in c.1736. It was occupied by an apothecary in 1705, and was certainly a chemist from 1826 to recent times.

St.Michael's Church   159/60   161   162   163/4   165   166   167   168

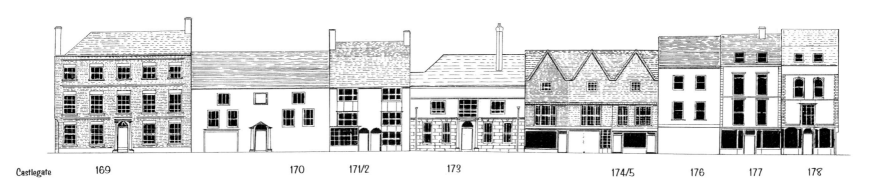

Castlegate   169   170   171/2   173   174/5   176   177   178

17

South side. From no. 78 to Keere Street

Nos. 78-81. These were the stables of the Stewards Inn.

Nos. 78-9. Built (perhaps as three in 1777 including no. 77 above) by the widow of Dr Richard Russell, who popularised sea bathing at Brighton.

Nos. 80/1. These were built between 1753 and 1766. No. 80 was re-numbered nos. 80-81 after 1812. All numbers west of this house have been shifted by one number. Not all commentators have noticed this adjustment.

St. Swithun's Lane

No. 82. Newly built by William Michell in 1773 on the site of a smaller building. One of the finest of Lewes' Georgian buildings.

No. 83. Was an Inn called The Bell from c.1593 to 1683. The name may commemorate the casting of a bell for St.Michaels church. The present building dates to 1816.

Nos. 84/5. Destroyed by fire in 1904 and re-built in the present form. The inset diagram is based on Walter Godfrey's notes, and shows its predecessors.

No. 86. A part of it was an Inn called The Cat before 1623.

Nos. 87/8 . St Michael's House. One house, in single ownership to 1784, it may have been part of the property of Christchurch, Canterbury. There are fine stone mullioned windows at rear.

BOTTOM LINE

Nos. 89-90. Built 1806, the earlier buildings having been demolished.

No. 91. The Brewers Arms. So named in 1800, but previously known as The Ship and before that the Red Lion from about 1690. Re-built to its present appearance in about 1897. The inset shows (following Walter Godfrey's drawing) the previous building.

No. 92. The Bull Inn. This could be fifteenth century. It is overshadowed by the bulk of the town house of Sir Henry Goring behind (built c.1583), later the Westgate Chapel. The Bull Inn is the administrative headquarters of the Sussex Archaeological Society.

No. 93. Westgate House. The site of the south bastion of the Westgate. This was built about 1785, and the eastern part was a shop until c.1950. The residential part was G.F. Harwood's preparatory school c.1890 to1910.

Nos. 96/8. The site was sold in 1736 to be repaired or re-built. The present triple building dates from 1795.

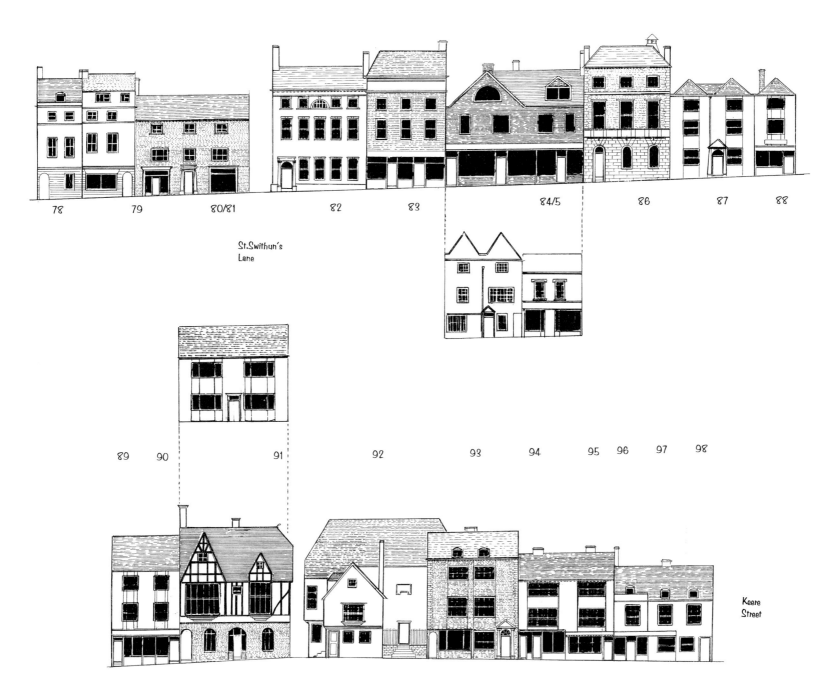

78   79   80/81   82   83   84/5   86   87   88

St.Swithun's
Lane

89   90   91   92   93   94   95 96   97   98

Keere
Street

19

From Keere Street to no. 109 High Street.

Nos. 99-100. The only remaining exposed timber-framed exterior in Lewes. Many other Lewes buildings have inside their exteriors a frame such as this. Here the frame is a re-construction of even earlier elements. The original building was plastered, thus covering over a lack of refinement in the earlier work. In the early 1900s the plaster was stripped and the frame re-exposed. The milestone in the facade was reset here when the building opposite was demolished.

No. 101. The last house in StMichaels Parish, south side, although it has (see below) been in StAnnes too. Owned in 1624 by Brian Twine, and latterly by his father Thomas Twine MD (there is a memorial in St Annes Church). Brian Twine was instrumental in drawing up the statutes of the University of Oxford.

Nos. 102-3. Held of the Manor of Plumpton, a sixteenth century building with a later front.

No. 104. Antioch House. Held of Plumpton Manor. Named after the lost Antioch Street (to Southover), which was its western border. Previous owners included Richard Broughton, an MP for Lewes c.1658. Again, a Georgian front hides an earlier structure.

BOTTOM LINE

Nos. 105-7. The earliest origins of this group of three is not yet understood.

Antioch Street (Originally a street communicating with Southover)

Nos. 108-9. Built c.1824, originally three but now only two remain. Built in the cemetery of St Peter Westout, and also probably on the site of Sherman's Chantry Chapel.

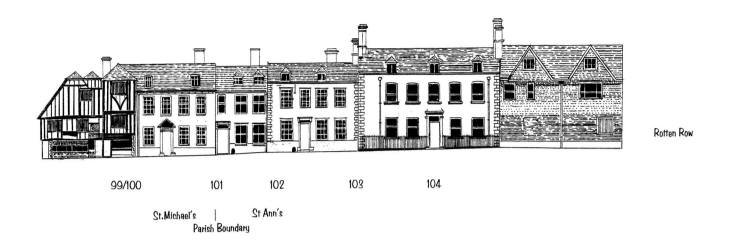

Rotten Row

99/100   101   102   103   104

St. Michael's | St Ann's
Parish Boundary

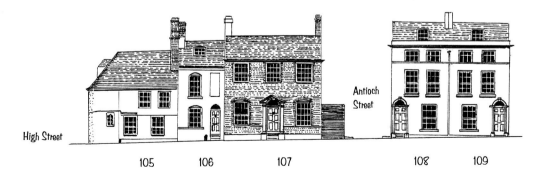

Antioch
Street

High Street

105   106   107   108   109

21

SHEET ELEVEN.

North side. St Anne's Hill. From the Old Grammar School to no. 157 High Street.

The old Free School moved here from Southover after being given this property in 1718. The Free School eventually closed and the present school is a successor in name, the property being an 1851 re-building, remarkable for its very high standard of knapped flint facade. The building stands partly on the site of Sherman's Chantry House, let to provide an income for his Chantry Chapel in the cemetery opposite.

Nos. 138-9. One building, divided into two in 1834, which thus shifted street numbers one digit eastwards. From 1792 to 1834 it was the home and business address of W.B. Langridge, Lewes solicitor and Sussex Clerk of the Peace, an indefatigable developer of Lewes property on his own and other people's account.

No. 139 is fronted in fine knapped flint, and dated 1654 on the rainwater head. This may reflect an earlier separation.

Nos. 140-1. As an example of continuity, the Stonestreat family owned and occupied parts of these two properties from before 1570 up to 1713. 141 was the King's Head, a seventeenth century inn, and may have been the 'Black Boy', not the Black Dog as some have claimed, before then. In 1851 it was being used as the poor house of the parish of StAnne.

No. 142. Another of the many examples of a Georgian front covering an earlier structure.

No. 143. This prominent building, and its predecessor, seem to occupy a copyhold site intended to frustrate a direct attack down St.Anne's Hill to the medieval West Gate. The site was a collection of buildings and gardens (including an Inn called the White Horse until it moved to nos. 165-7). In 1624 it was held by Thomas Rowe and occupied by his brother John Rowe, on whose labour so much of the sort of knowledge used in this publication depends. Later the property came into the possession of a family called Newdigate. It has been denied that there is any connection with the Sir Roger Newdigate who founded a poetry prize at Oxford University, but one of that rank and name was involved in the sale in 1747/8.

BOTTOM LINE

Nos. 144-5. These small cottages (shown inset) were demolished and nos. 144 and 5 replaced them. The milestone from London, now in the front of nos. 99/100 opposite, came from no. 145 originally.

Westgate Street, (Once Cutler's Bars).

Nos. 148-50. Now the Freemason's Hall (built 1868-72) it occupies the northern bastion of the West Gate. The date stone says 1797, but this refers to the Freemasons, not the current building.

Pipe Passage (leads to the base of the Town Mill, erected in 1800 for the benefit of the poor.

Nos. 151-5. The western part (no. 151) is older than the rest, which must date from after 1735, when it was bought by the Pelhams.

Nos. 156-7. These two little cottages were demolished about 1881, when the church hall of St Michaels was built. The old market clock, then in the clock house at the church, was moved here and is still in situ.

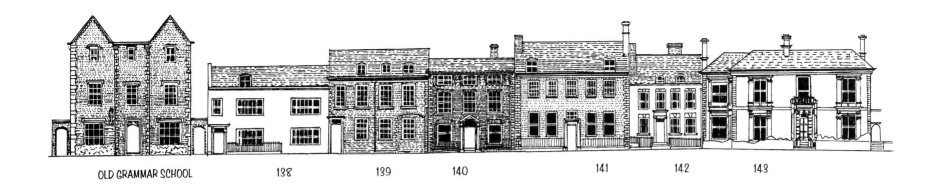

OLD GRAMMAR SCHOOL   138   139   140   141   142   143

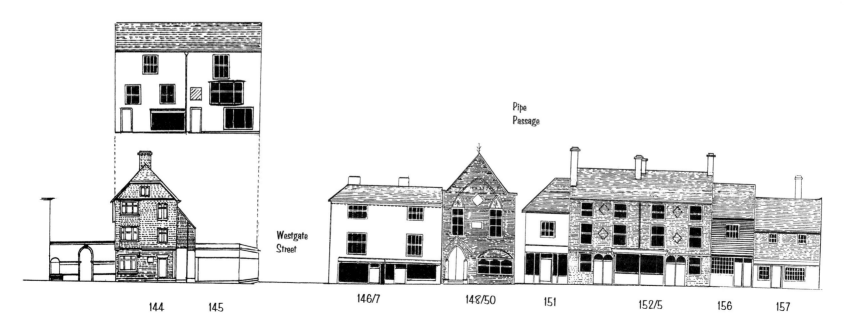

Pipe
Passage

Westgate
Street

144   145   146/7   148/50   151   152/5   156   157

23

St Anne's Hill (High Street) South side, from no. 110 to Church Lane at no. 125.

TOP LINE

No. 110. This was the site of the church of St Peter Westout and its cemetery, but which after the union with the parish of St.Mary (now collectively known as St Anne,) had became the Rectory (of St Peters) by 1615, and then StAnne's Parsonage. The present building dates to c.1800. In 1790, before the older buildings on the site were demolished, they were occupied by Miss Lund and later Miss Ryall, who ran ladies schools. Remains of stone from the old structures can be seen in the walls in front of the first houses in Rotten Row.

Nos. 111-114. No. 111 was the site of a house barn and croft of 1.5 acres which accounted for much of the south side of St Annes Hill. The building dates from 1719, although it has been updated since. Among many owners and occupiers were Sir Thomas Woodcock and the Earl of Abergavenny, who sold to John Apsley in 1719, and continued, (in part by a union of the Apsley & Dalrymple families), in that ownership until 1803. Nos. 112-4 were built in the croft of no. 111. There were four small houses here in 1691, but by 1717 these were newly built as three. No. 112 was demolished in 1754.

BOTTOM LINE

Nos. 115-7. Three pleasant houses of c.1750 were bought by the Duke of Newcastle in 1737 and sold by the Pelhams in 1809 to raise money to pay off Newcastle's legacy of debt.

No. 118. Hill Lodge. This is a fine house built before 1676 by William Spence. It was held by the Spence family until sold by Luke Spence in 1771 (and perhaps re-fronted) then to the Rev Robert Austin, Rector of St Annes.

No. 119. Once called Dorrington House. A Georgian re-building of three small tenements.

No. 120. Probably originally part of the three tenements above. Mathematical tiles over a timber frame. It is not listed in the Borough rentals. It is difficult to recognise the 1884 claim, continued to the present day, that they were once the Rectory of St.Michaels.

Nos. 121-3. These were the poor house of St Annes parish in 1735, and the Church House before then. The passageway in the middle of the frontage led through to two further houses in the grounds, demolished in 1831.

Nos. 124-5. A house built on the site of the manor pound. In 1735 these were a barn of two bays, in 1773 two houses and workshops, and became three houses (with an extension of no. 125) in 1817/18.

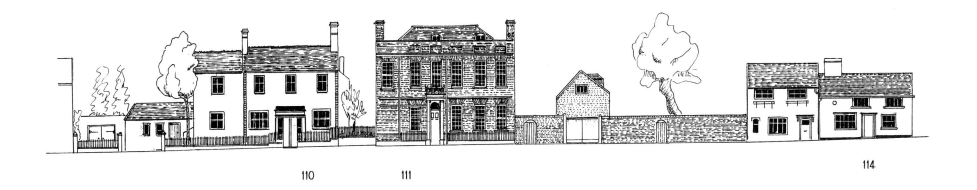

110   111   114

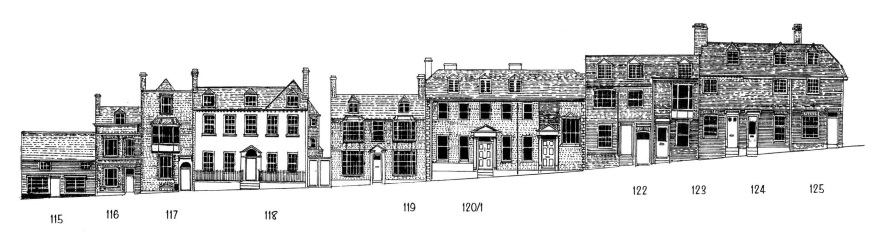

115   116   117   118   119   120/1   122   123   124   125

SHEET THIRTEEN. TOP LINE

Not numbered

St Pancras Church. The plot was occupied as tenements and a barn by John Ireland in the 1570s, and gave the name to Irelands Lane, the westernmost limit of the later Borough. The first religious services were held in 1872, but the present church was built in 1939.

Pelham Arms. Known as the Dog in the mid eighteenth century, had been bought by Thomas Pelham-Holles, Duke of Newcastle by 1732. The name was changed about 1790.

Well House Place.

This seems always to have been crossed by a public passage from the High Street to the Wall Lands on the north, from before the time that Irelands Lane was created. It was 'The Slipp or Wellfied' in 1770, the Wellhouse in 1790 and the Well Croft in 1794.

Nos. 127-9. The Lord's Houses in c.1570, these three (with nos. 130/31 below) had been re-developed by 1812.

No. 128. This has a modern front, and was said to have been an inn called the Morning Star up to the beginning of the twentieth century.

Nos. 130-131. The double number is unexplained. In 1570 this property was called The Hermitage and may refer to a building let to provide maintenance for the anchoress in St Mary's church.

St Peter's Place. (1868, a development by the Neville family.)

Nos. 132-4. Known as The Rose (which may not necessarily have been an inn name) in the seventeenth century, the present houses are a composite. An earlier house on this site was known as Hankynges.

BOTTOM LINE

No. 134. The later name Millers recognises the ownership in 1825 by a miller. A public passage to Paddock Lane formed the eastern boundary.

Nos. 135-6. Two stables and a close in 1596, by 1609 it housed (amongst others) a Smith's forge and workshop. When developed to its present appearance in 1738 it lost part of the eastern side of no. 136 to Shelley's Hotel.

Not numbered

Shelley's Hotel.

The earliest reference dates to 1526, when it was a hostelry called The Vine. It was bought as a private house in 1596/7 by Thomas Sackville, Lord Buckhurst, and bought by Henry Shelley in 1663. A successor re-modelled the street elevation without altering the porch of 1570, which bears the earliest known owners initials.